Genre Realistic F

Essential Questio
What kinds of challeng...   .... people.

by Susan Paris
illustrated by Aleksandar Sotirovski

Chapter 1 Baggage

Frankie sat on the sofa, trying to concentrate. It was difficult with her younger brother, Lee, hovering at the opposite end, expressing his frustration.

Thwack! Thwack! Thwack! Lee's tennis racket connected with the upholstery, releasing a puff of dust each time. Hitting the sofa was obviously satisfying, and Frankie resolved to say nothing. If she kept reading quietly, her brother might give up and go away.

No such luck.

"You don't *have* to come, you know," Lee whispered crossly. "Why don't you spend the day with Audrey? It's not too late."

It was a good option. Frankie didn't even want to go on the hiking trip. A few months ago, Dad had suggested taking Lee and his friends on a day trip to Rocky Mountain National Park. It was meant to be boys only, but then Mom had decided at the last minute to go to a conference, which meant she couldn't take Frankie to the aquarium, and that left Frankie stranded. Not only that, but now she was baggage—her brother's unwanted baggage, and no doubt his friends' too.

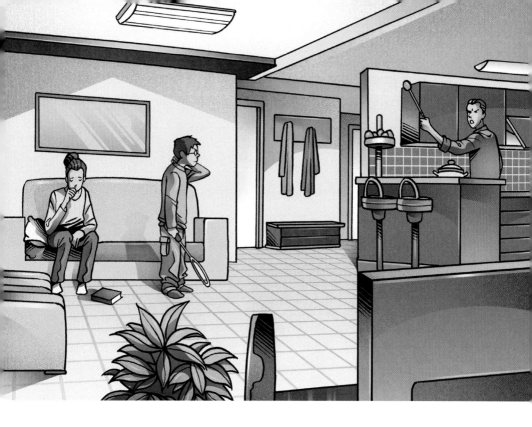

"I'll get you the phone," Lee said, remaining persistent but speaking quietly so Dad wouldn't hear.

It didn't work.

"Lee!" Dad called from the kitchen. "We've discussed this. Frankie's coming hiking, and that's final."

Frankie banged her book shut. Now she was mad, too. Had Dad bothered to ask if she wanted to come? No, he'd just assumed she'd go along, when the truth was she'd much rather sit here *reading* about hiking in Rocky Mountain National Park than actually doing it. She didn't want to spend the day with her brother and his juvenile friends, she didn't want to clump around in hiking boots, and most of all, she didn't want to meet any bears.

Lee's friends Damien and Adam didn't seem surprised to find Frankie standing by the car the next morning. No doubt Lee had sent them texts complaining about her.

Dad turned to them and said, "Listen up. You need to take responsibility for your own gear. Check that you have water, food, spare clothing, and a raincoat." Frankie and the boys dutifully checked their gear.

Dad's own kit was comprehensive: compass, survival blanket, first-aid kit, extra water, matches, and more. He checked his supplies while Frankie watched.

Finally they were ready to go. Lee slid into the back seat next to his friends, trailing his headphones behind him. The three boys immediately started listening to music and snorting at the occasional joke that passed between them. "I bet they wouldn't notice if Dad were driving them to the moon," Frankie thought. She was the only one looking at the changing scenery out the window. Dad followed her gaze, pleased that she seemed interested.

"Look at that!" he said and waved his arm in a general way to include everything outside the car.

"What?" Frankie said. "There's nothing there."

"Exactly!" Dad said. "No malls, no traffic jams, just us and the great outdoors."

STOP AND CHECK

Why does Frankie have to go on the hike with her younger brother?

Chapter 2 The Real Deal

Dad insisted their hiking experience must be the "real deal," so he had chosen one of the least popular hiking routes, leaving from the foot of an isolated road. By the time they reached the small parking lot, it was mid-morning and there were few people around. The weather was drizzly and overcast, which seemed to please Dad even more.

"We'll have the place to ourselves," he said, dumping his gear on the ground.

"No kidding," Adam said, peering around like he'd been shaken awake from a dream. "Where is everyone?"

Frankie was wondering the same thing, but all she said to her dad was, "Do you have a map?"

"Of course. Let's take a look. I'll show you where we're headed." Frankie and her dad studied the map while the boys goofed around and drifted toward the trailhead.

It was still drizzling when they set out—the boys racing ahead, followed by Dad and Frankie. The trail stretched before them, disappearing into the forest like a path in a fairy tale.

"Wait up," Dad hollered. "We need to stick together."

Frankie and Dad found the boys around the next curve, looking as though they'd been waiting all morning.

"What's the problem?" Lee asked, clearly irked. "There's a trail. We won't get lost."

"Safety in numbers," Dad said.

"Safety from what?" Frankie asked suspiciously.

"Bears," Adam said. "They're all over these woods."

Frankie *knew* it. She knew she should have made a fuss about this trip and gone to her friend Audrey's house instead.

"They're just black bears," Damien said. "They'll leave you alone if you're careful."

"That's right," Dad said. "Never approach one, and make lots of noise when you're hiking so you don't startle one. If you do see one, tell me right away."

"Got that, Frankie? Make sure you tell Dad right before you start running from those big bear claws and those big bear teeth." As he said this, Lee pretended to swipe at Frankie with his outstretched arms, and he opened his mouth wide in a snarl.

In spite of herself, Frankie jumped, and Lee and the other boys laughed at her.

"That's enough, Lee," Dad said sternly.

"Awww, I was just joking, Dad."

"Come on, boys," Dad said. "We're here to hike, and this time, I'd like Frankie to lead the way."

"Do I have to?" Frankie asked. "I don't want to be in the front."

"Fine!" Dad said. "I'll set the pace, but let's get going."

They climbed steadily, the day brightening around them, until eventually even Adam stopped talking. All around, there was nothing but trees, the occasional hawk, the bright-blue sky overhead, and intermittent glimpses of the magnificent Mummy Ranges—not that Frankie was enjoying the view. She was concentrating on keeping up and on not stumbling on the rocks strewn across the trail. So far, she was doing okay, and most importantly, they hadn't seen any large, hairy beasts.

When they reached an alpine meadow, Dad announced it was lunchtime. They had climbed surprisingly high, and Frankie shrugged off her backpack and gazed at the vastness of the landscape surrounding her.

"Amazing, huh?" Damien said, coming up beside her.

"Bear country," Lee said in a deep, growly voice.

"Will you be *quiet*?" Frankie said. She was feeling frightened enough as it was, and she didn't need her brother reminding her of the possible danger.

"Let's all eat in peace," Dad suggested.

"Fantastic," Adam said. "I hope there's a ton of food!" He peered at the contents of a sandwich and recoiled in mock horror. "Hey, what's that green stuff?"

"Sprouts," Lee said glumly. "Dad grows them in a jar."

"They taste like grass, or maybe hay," Damien said.

"Your dad thinks we're horses," Adam said, neighing and pawing at the ground while the other boys howled with laughter.

"That's so not funny," Frankie muttered. "Hanging out with Lee has really skewed your sense of humor, Adam."

STOP AND CHECK

Why was Frankie anxious about the hike?

Chapter 3 The Accident

After lunch, Frankie trailed behind, determined to put some distance between herself and the boys. Dad, however, insisted that she stay within sight at all times.

When they came across a big rock, she was happy to stop. Her boots felt hot and uncomfortable, one of her socks was twisted, and she had a blister forming.

While sticking a bandage on her heel, Frankie watched Adam clamber up the rock, closely followed by Lee and Damien. Dad carefully pulled himself up after the boys, but as he went to stand up, the corner of the rock crumbled, and he lost his balance. Although he fell only a short distance, he landed awkwardly—and hard. Frankie heard the air go out of him before he mustered another breath to yell.

"Dad fell!" Frankie shouted, her voice edged with tears.

Lee's anxious face appeared over the edge of the rock. "I'm coming down," he said as he quickly but carefully climbed back to the ground.

Dad had his right arm crossed over his chest, holding on to his left shoulder. His face was such a mask of pain that Frankie found it difficult to look at him.

"Dad?" she said. "Dad, are you all right?"

"I'm okay," he murmured.

"Let's help him up," Lee said, rushing forward.

"No way," Frankie said. "We don't know what's wrong yet. It looks like his shoulder, but it could also be his neck, his back—anything."

"It's my shoulder," Dad said feebly.

"Does anything else hurt?" Frankie asked.

"My head, but not as bad."

Frankie crouched and took her father's hand. It was cold, and she could barely feel his return squeeze.

Frankie knew she needed to take charge, and almost immediately, she felt a calmness and strength she had not known she possessed.

"We need the survival blanket," Frankie said firmly.

"The what?" Lee asked.

"The silver blanket in Dad's backpack. People in shock get cold, and the blanket keeps them warm."

"How do you know that?" Lee asked.

"I read about hiking safety yesterday," Frankie said. "It's important we keep him warm, still, and comfortable."

"I'll go for help," Adam said. "There's that ranger station we passed before we got to the parking lot. It's not that far, and we can call emergency services from there."

Before anyone could reply, Dad roused himself, or tried to, but the effort was obviously too much, and he dropped back down. It occurred to Frankie that he probably needed water and maybe painkillers as well.

Adam was already rummaging through Dad's gear. "Got it," he cried, unfolding the map he'd found. "Look— this route is way shorter. It's not a marked trail, but I can always follow one of these streams if I get lost. See, there are tons of them."

"Good idea, Adam," Lee said. "The sooner we get down the mountain, the better."

Was it a good idea? Frankie couldn't remember tons of streams. In fact, she could remember only two. She peered more closely as Adam's finger traced his planned route.

"If you mean those lines, they're not streams," Frankie said, pointing to the map. "They're contour lines."

"Contour lines show altitude—that's how high you are above sea level," she continued. "Dad showed me when we studied the map back in the parking lot."

"It still looks like a quicker route to me," Adam said.

Frankie knew she had to summon the courage to stop Adam from turning their dilemma into a disaster. "If you get hurt or stuck or something, Dad won't be rescued."

Adam drew back his foot and sent a stone scuttling across the clearing. Other than a muffled knock as it hit a tree trunk, there was silence.

In the end, Damien broke the stalemate. "Frankie's right," he said. "It's safer to go back the way we came."

Dad groaned, and Frankie felt a jolt of fear run through her. Someone needed to leave to find help now, and she needed to look after her father. The thought of bears crept back into her mind—there was no way she was staying there alone.

"One of you *is* staying with me," she said to put a stop to any more arguments. "We should split into two groups of two for safety," she added.

"Let me guess—you read that too?" Adam said, but Damien quickly argued that Frankie's idea made the most sense.

It seemed there was nothing more to decide, so Lee and Adam repacked one backpack and drank some water.

"Make sure you take something to eat," Frankie said, "and take the map with you."

"Man, your sister goes on and on!" Adam grumbled as the two boys prepared to go.

"Tell me about it," Lee said, but he gave Frankie an embarrassed smile before he disappeared from sight.

There wasn't much to do after Lee and Adam left. Frankie adjusted the blanket around her dad and gave him water regularly while Damien watched for Lee and Adam's return.

"I wonder how much longer before they get back," Frankie said nervously a while later.

Damien came to sit beside her while she tended to her father. "It's faster going downhill than uphill," he said reassuringly.

Not too much later, Lee and Adam were back with a park ranger they'd met partway down the mountain. The ranger checked Dad and announced that he'd be fine.

"It's lucky I was on the trail today," the ranger said. "I've radioed for a helicopter, and it's on its way."

Then the ranger turned to Frankie. "I also hear it's lucky you were with your father today. Your brother told me you took charge and kept a cool head." Lee looked at his sister sheepishly.

Frankie smiled shyly. "I'm not so good with bears, but I think I've got this hiking thing covered."

STOP AND CHECK

What events help Frankie feel good by the end of the story?

Respond to Reading

Summarize

Use important details from *Bear Country* to summarize how Frankie was transformed by her challenge. Information from your graphic organizer may help.

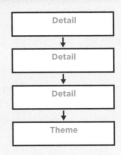

Text Evidence

1. How do you know that this is realistic fiction? **GENRE**

2. What challenge brings about a change in Frankie? **THEME**

3. What does *isolated* on page 5 mean? Read the paragraph that contains the word to find clues. **PARAGRAPH CLUES**

4. Use details from Chapter 3 to write about how Frankie's actions show what the author's main message is. **WRITE ABOUT READING**

Compare Texts

Read about a girl who had to find the strength to meet a challenge.

I knew I shouldn't do it. It was a real dilemma, but when you're with friends—or more accurately, people whom you *want* as friends—bad ideas can seem like okay ideas. Sometimes, if you don't let yourself think about it carefully, they can even seem like good ideas.

Laura, Rachel, Emily, and I were about to play a "game" called Who Can Stay on the Phone the Longest. Not so difficult, but there was a twist—the person on the other end had to be a complete stranger. Laura held the record at five minutes, forty seconds … supposedly.

Now it was my turn, and I was petrified. I'd never made a prank call before, and I didn't particularly want to start now. Rachel gave me a sympathetic look.

"Do you want a glass of milk?" she asked.

I shook my head because right then, even thinking of eating or drinking anything made me feel sick.

Laura waggled the phone at me and raised her eyebrows questioningly. She was used to calling the shots while everyone rushed around desperately seeking her approval. Last semester, I hadn't cared what Laura thought of me because I hadn't needed to care. I'd had Nina then, but now that Nina had switched schools, things were different.

I wiped my hands on my jeans and reached for the phone. It was surprisingly easy to dial the number. Knowing I had made my decision and was sticking with it, I didn't let myself think about the consequences. The phone rang, and a familiar voice answered right away, just as if she'd been waiting for me.

"Hey, Nina," I said, "it's me ..."

Laura was flicking through a magazine when I finished my conversation with Nina ten minutes later. "You broke the rules. Very disappointing," she said.

"I couldn't do it," I said. "I think it's a really bad idea."

"*We've* all done it," Laura said smugly.

Suddenly I doubted it. "Have you *really*?" I asked.

"Actually," Rachel said, "I haven't, and Emily hung up after two seconds, remember?"

18

Emily spoke up. "I didn't want to give some stranger a bad day. I agree that it's a stupid game anyway."

There was silence while Laura held our gaze, waiting … but she seemed uncertain. The best option was to change the subject, only I couldn't think what to say.

Then Laura surprised me by changing the subject herself. "What's Nina's new school like?" she asked.

"Okay," I said, "but she doesn't know anyone yet."

"You guys must really miss each other," Laura said.

"Well, you have us now," Rachel said.

"Totally true," Emily added.

And maybe I did.

Make Connections

What change did the narrator's decision bring about in her challenging situation? ESSENTIAL QUESTION

In both stories, characters have to speak up for what they know is right. Compare the ways Frankie in *Bear Country* and the girl in *The Call* deal with these challenges. TEXT TO TEXT

Focus on Literary Elements

Simile A simile is a way of describing one thing by comparing it with another. Authors use similes to make vivid descriptions. When you're reading, a simile can help you better understand what is being described.

Read and Find Similes often start with the words *like a* or *as a*. Here are some examples: "He turned red as a beet." "She swam like a dolphin." "Joey was as quiet as a mouse."

On page 5 of *Bear Country*, the author writes that Adam peers around "like he'd been shaken awake from a dream." Also on page 5, the trail is "disappearing into the forest like a path in a fairy tale."

Your Turn

Have a simile challenge with a partner or in a group. Set a time limit, such as five minutes. Each person looks for places in the story where similes could make a description more dramatic. For example, describe how Frankie felt when she saw her dad fall.

When the time is up, read your similes to each other. Check that they describe one thing as being *like* or *as* something else.